THIS PLANNER BELONGS TO

2020 AT A GLANCE

JANUARY 2020

S	M	T	W	T	F	S
			1	2	3	4
5	6	7	8	9	10	11
12	13	14	15	16	17	18
19	20	21	22	23	24	25
26	27	28	29	30	31	

FEBRUARY 2020

S	M	T	W	T	F	S
						1
2	3	4	5	6	7	8
9	10	11	12	13	14	15
16	17	18	19	20	21	22
23	24	25	26	27	28	29

MARCH 2020

S	M	T	W	T	F	S
1	2	3	4	5	6	7
8	9	10	11	12	13	14
15	16	17	18	19	20	21
22	23	24	25	26	27	28
29	30	31				

APRIL 2020

S	M	T	W	T	F	S
			1	2	3	4
5	6	7	8	9	10	11
12	13	14	15	16	17	18
19	20	21	22	23	24	25
26	27	28	29	30		

MAY 2020

S	M	T	W	T	F	S
					1	2
3	4	5	6	7	8	9
10	11	12	13	14	15	16
17	18	19	20	21	22	23
24/31	25	26	27	28	29	30

JUNE 2020

S	M	T	W	T	F	S
	1	2	3	4	5	6
7	8	9	10	11	12	13
14	15	16	17	18	19	20
21	22	23	24	25	26	27
28	29	30				

JULY 2020

S	M	T	W	T	F	S
			1	2	3	4
5	6	7	8	9	10	11
12	13	14	15	16	17	18
19	20	21	22	23	24	25
26	27	28	29	30	31	

AUGUST 2020

S	M	T	W	T	F	S
						1
2	3	4	5	6	7	8
9	10	11	12	13	14	15
16	17	18	19	20	21	22
23/30	24/31	25	26	27	28	29

SEPTEMBER 2020

S	M	T	W	T	F	S
		1	2	3	4	5
6	7	8	9	10	11	12
13	14	15	16	17	18	19
20	21	22	23	24	25	26
27	28	29	30			

OCTOBER 2020

S	M	T	W	T	F	S
				1	2	3
4	5	6	7	8	9	10
11	12	13	14	15	16	17
18	19	20	21	22	23	24
25	26	27	28	29	30	31

NOVEMBER 2020

S	M	T	W	T	F	S
1	2	3	4	5	6	7
8	9	10	11	12	13	14
15	16	17	18	19	20	21
22	23	24	25	26	27	28
29	30					

DECEMBER 2020

S	M	T	W	T	F	S
		1	2	3	4	5
6	7	8	9	10	11	12
13	14	15	16	17	18	19
20	21	22	23	24	25	26
27	28	29	30	31		

2021 AT A GLANCE

JANUARY 2021

S	M	T	W	T	F	S
					1	2
3	4	5	6	7	8	9
10	11	12	13	14	15	16
17	18	19	20	21	22	23
24/31	25	26	27	28	29	30

FEBRUARY 2021

S	M	T	W	T	F	S
	1	2	3	4	5	6
7	8	9	10	11	12	13
14	15	16	17	18	19	20
21	22	23	24	25	26	27
28						

MARCH 2021

S	M	T	W	T	F	S
	1	2	3	4	5	6
7	8	9	10	11	12	13
14	15	16	17	18	19	20
21	22	23	24	25	26	27
28	29	30	31			

APRIL 2021

S	M	T	W	T	F	S
				1	2	3
4	5	6	7	8	9	10
11	12	13	14	15	16	17
18	19	20	21	22	23	24
25	26	27	28	29	30	

MAY 2021

S	M	T	W	T	F	S
						1
2	3	4	5	6	7	8
9	10	11	12	13	14	15
16	17	18	19	20	21	22
23/30	24/31	25	26	27	28	29

JUNE 2021

S	M	T	W	T	F	S
		1	2	3	4	5
6	7	8	9	10	11	12
13	14	15	16	17	18	19
20	21	22	23	24	25	26
27	28	29	30			

JULY 2021

S	M	T	W	T	F	S
				1	2	3
4	5	6	7	8	9	10
11	12	13	14	15	16	17
18	19	20	21	22	23	24
25	26	27	28	29	30	31

AUGUST 2021

S	M	T	W	T	F	S
1	2	3	4	5	6	7
8	9	10	11	12	13	14
15	16	17	18	19	20	21
22	23	24	25	26	27	28
29	30	31				

SEPTEMBER 2021

S	M	T	W	T	F	S
			1	2	3	4
5	6	7	8	9	10	11
12	13	14	15	16	17	18
19	20	21	22	23	24	25
26	27	28	29	30		

OCTOBER 2021

S	M	T	W	T	F	S
					1	2
3	4	5	6	7	8	9
10	11	12	13	14	15	16
17	18	19	20	21	22	23
24/31	25	26	27	28	29	30

NOVEMBER 2021

S	M	T	W	T	F	S
	1	2	3	4	5	6
7	8	9	10	11	12	13
14	15	16	17	18	19	20
21	22	23	24	25	26	27
28	29	30				

DECEMBER 2021

S	M	T	W	T	F	S
			1	2	3	4
5	6	7	8	9	10	11
12	13	14	15	16	17	18
19	20	21	22	23	24	25
26	27	28	29	30	31	

MONTHLY GOALS

NEW GOALS TO FOCUS ON

WHAT WORKED LAST MONTH

WHAT COULD BE BETTER

The Secret to Getting Ahead is Getting Started

AUGUST 2020

SUNDAY	MONDAY	TUESDAY	WEDNESDAY	THURSDAY	FRIDAY	SATURDAY
26	27	28	29	30	31	1
2	3 Summer Bank Holiday (SCT)	4	5	6	7	8
9	10	11	12	13	14	15
16	17	18	19	20	21	22
23/30	24/31 Summer Bank Holiday (31st: UK except SCT)	25	26	27	28	29

CREATURE OF HABIT

Track new goals or habits and watch your progress every month!

HABIT	1	2	3	4	5	6	7	8	9	10	11	12	13	14	15	16	17	18	19	20	21	22	23	24	25	26	27	28	29	30	31

2020 JULY/AUGUST

MONDAY
27

RISE AND SHINE!
TIME TO CHANGE THE WORLD!

TUESDAY
28

WEDNESDAY
29

DO GOOD. BE KIND. STAY YOU.

THURSDAY
30

LIFE MIGHT BE TOUGH,
BUT YOU'RE TOUGHER.

FRIDAY 31

SATURDAY 1

P.S. DON'T FORGET TO
HAVE A GOOD TIME.

SUNDAY 2

DON'T FORGET:

THIS WEEK'S
HAPPY MOMENT:

AUGUST 2020

S	M	T	W	T	F	S
						1
2	3	4	5	6	7	8
9	10	11	12	13	14	15
16	17	18	19	20	21	22
23/30	24/31	25	26	27	28	29

SEPTEMBER 2020

S	M	T	W	T	F	S
		1	2	3	4	5
6	7	8	9	10	11	12
13	14	15	16	17	18	19
20	21	22	23	24	25	26
27	28	29	30			

2020 **AUGUST**

MONDAY
3

Summer Bank Holiday (SCT)

TUESDAY
4

YOU ARE GREATER THAN YOU KNOW!

WEDNESDAY
5

THURSDAY
6

WHEN A NEW OBSTACLE COMES YOUR WAY,
SAY YES AND MAKE THE MOST OF IT.

FRIDAY
7

SATURDAY
8

HAPPY WEEKEND! THIS IS THE START OF ANYTHING YOU WANT.

SUNDAY
9

DON'T FORGET:

THIS WEEK'S HAPPY MOMENT:

AUGUST 2020

S	M	T	W	T	F	S
						1
2	3	4	5	6	7	8
9	10	11	12	13	14	15
16	17	18	19	20	21	22
23/30	24/31	25	26	27	28	29

SEPTEMBER 2020

S	M	T	W	T	F	S
		1	2	3	4	5
6	7	8	9	10	11	12
13	14	15	16	17	18	19
20	21	22	23	24	25	26
27	28	29	30			

2020 AUGUST

MONDAY
10

TODAY'S A GOOD DAY TO
SEE THE LIGHT IN EVERYTHING.

TUESDAY
11

WEDNESDAY
12

LIVE AND LOVE TO THE FULLEST!

THURSDAY
13

YOU DON'T HAVE TO FIX EVERYTHING.

FRIDAY
14

SATURDAY
15

DO SOMETHING TODAY YOU'LL NEVER FORGET.

SUNDAY
16

DON'T FORGET:

THIS WEEK'S HAPPY MOMENT:

AUGUST 2020

S	M	T	W	T	F	S
						1
2	3	4	5	6	7	8
9	10	11	12	13	14	15
16	17	18	19	20	21	22
23/30	24/31	25	26	27	28	29

SEPTEMBER 2020

S	M	T	W	T	F	S
		1	2	3	4	5
6	7	8	9	10	11	12
13	14	15	16	17	18	19
20	21	22	23	24	25	26
27	28	29	30			

2020 **AUGUST**

MONDAY
17

TUESDAY
18

NO MATTER WHAT LIFE THROWS AT YOU,
FIND A WAY TO HAVE FUN WITH IT!

WEDNESDAY
19

THURSDAY
20

WHAT WILL YOU DREAM UP NEXT?

FRIDAY
21

SATURDAY
22

EVERY
DAY IS A
SPECIAL
OCCASION!

SUNDAY
23

DON'T FORGET:

THIS WEEK'S
HAPPY MOMENT:

AUGUST 2020

S	M	T	W	T	F	S
						1
2	3	4	5	6	7	8
9	10	11	12	13	14	15
16	17	18	19	20	21	22
23/30	24/31	25	26	27	28	29

SEPTEMBER 2020

S	M	T	W	T	F	S
		1	2	3	4	5
6	7	8	9	10	11	12
13	14	15	16	17	18	19
20	21	22	23	24	25	26
27	28	29	30			

2020 **AUGUST**

BE CREATIVE AND HAVE FUN!

MONDAY
24

TUESDAY
25

TRY HARD EVERY DAY.

WEDNESDAY
26

THURSDAY
27

STRESS? HA! LAUGH IN ITS FACE!

FRIDAY
28

SATURDAY
29

BREW A CUP OF TEA AND HEAD OVER TO YOUR CALM, HAPPY PLACE.

SUNDAY
30

DON'T FORGET:

THIS WEEK'S HAPPY MOMENT:

AUGUST 2020

S	M	T	W	T	F	S
						1
2	3	4	5	6	7	8
9	10	11	12	13	14	15
16	17	18	19	20	21	22
23/30	24/31	25	26	27	28	29

SEPTEMBER 2020

S	M	T	W	T	F	S
		1	2	3	4	5
6	7	8	9	10	11	12
13	14	15	16	17	18	19
20	21	22	23	24	25	26
27	28	29	30			

MONTHLY GOALS

NEW GOALS TO FOCUS ON

WHAT WORKED LAST MONTH

WHAT COULD BE BETTER

it's
time
to
shine

SEPTEMBER 2020

SUNDAY	MONDAY	TUESDAY	WEDNESDAY	THURSDAY	FRIDAY	SATURDAY
30	31	1	2	3	4	5
6 Father's Day (AUS, NZ)	7 Labor Day (USA, CAN)	8	9	10	11 Patriot Day	12
13	14	15	16	17	18 Rosh Hashanah begins	19
20	21	22 Autumn begins (Northern Hemisphere)	23	24	25	26
27 Yom Kippur begins	28	29	30	1	2	3

CREATURE OF HABIT

Track new goals or habits and watch your progress every month!

HABIT	1	2	3	4	5	6	7	8	9	10	11	12	13	14	15	16	17	18	19	20	21	22	23	24	25	26	27	28	29	30	31

2020 AUGUST/SEPTEMBER

MONDAY
31

Summer Bank Holiday (UK except SCT)

TUESDAY
1

SHOW OFF THAT INVINCIBLE SPIRIT!
YOU'VE EARNED A RIGHT TO BRAG.

WEDNESDAY
2

THURSDAY
3

YOU'RE NOT WEIRD.
YOU'RE LIMITED EDITION!

FRIDAY
4

WHO CARES IF IT RAINS TODAY? YOU KNOW A RAINBOW IS COMING.

SATURDAY
5

SUNDAY
6

Father's Day (AUS, NZ)

DON'T FORGET:

THIS WEEK'S HAPPY MOMENT:

SEPTEMBER 2020

S	M	T	W	T	F	S
		1	2	3	4	5
6	7	8	9	10	11	12
13	14	15	16	17	18	19
20	21	22	23	24	25	26
27	28	29	30			

OCTOBER 2020

S	M	T	W	T	F	S
				1	2	3
4	5	6	7	8	9	10
11	12	13	14	15	16	17
18	19	20	21	22	23	24
25	26	27	28	29	30	31

2020 SEPTEMBER

MONDAY
7

WAKE UP, STRETCH, AND
START YOUR DAY OFF RIGHT!

Labor Day (USA, CAN)

TUESDAY
8

WEDNESDAY
9

DON'T LET A BAD DAY YESTERDAY
RUIN A GOOD DAY TODAY.

THURSDAY
10

ANYTHING WORTH DOING
IS WORTH OVERDOING.

FRIDAY 11

Patriot Day

SATURDAY 12

NEVER SELL YOURSELF SHORT.

SUNDAY 13

DON'T FORGET:

THIS WEEK'S HAPPY MOMENT:

SEPTEMBER 2020

S	M	T	W	T	F	S
		1	2	3	4	5
6	7	8	9	10	11	12
13	14	15	16	17	18	19
20	21	22	23	24	25	26
27	28	29	30			

OCTOBER 2020

S	M	T	W	T	F	S
				1	2	3
4	5	6	7	8	9	10
11	12	13	14	15	16	17
18	19	20	21	22	23	24
25	26	27	28	29	30	31

2020 SEPTEMBER

MONDAY
14

TUESDAY
15

EVEN AFTER EVERYTHING,
YOU CAN STILL MAKE SPACE FOR HOPE.

WEDNESDAY
16

THURSDAY
17

NORMAL IS OVERRATED.
HOW WILL YOU BE UNIQUE?

FRIDAY
18

Rosh Hashanah begins

SAY YES
TO NEW
ADVENTURES!

SATURDAY
19

SUNDAY
20

DON'T FORGET:

THIS WEEK'S
HAPPY MOMENT:

SEPTEMBER 2020

S	M	T	W	T	F	S
		1	2	3	4	5
6	7	8	9	10	11	12
13	14	15	16	17	18	19
20	21	22	23	24	25	26
27	28	29	30			

OCTOBER 2020

S	M	T	W	T	F	S
				1	2	3
4	5	6	7	8	9	10
11	12	13	14	15	16	17
18	19	20	21	22	23	24
25	26	27	28	29	30	31

2020 SEPTEMBER

MONDAY
21

REMEMBER: TOMORROW IS A NEW DAY.

TUESDAY
22

Autumn begins (Northern Hemisphere)

WEDNESDAY
23

LEAVES ARE FALLING, AND AUTUMN IS CALLING! SAVOR IT.

THURSDAY
24

BREAKING NEWS: YOU'RE MARVELOUS!

FRIDAY
25

SATURDAY
26

LAUGHS ARE CONTAGIOUS. SHARE THEM!

SUNDAY
27

Yom Kippur begins

DON'T FORGET:

THIS WEEK'S HAPPY MOMENT:

SEPTEMBER 2020

S	M	T	W	T	F	S
		1	2	3	4	5
6	7	8	9	10	11	12
13	14	15	16	17	18	19
20	21	22	23	24	25	26
27	28	29	30			

OCTOBER 2020

S	M	T	W	T	F	S
				1	2	3
4	5	6	7	8	9	10
11	12	13	14	15	16	17
18	19	20	21	22	23	24
25	26	27	28	29	30	31

MONTHLY GOALS

NEW GOALS TO FOCUS ON

WHAT WORKED LAST MONTH

WHAT COULD BE BETTER

DON'T WORRY. BE HAPPY!

OCTOBER 2020

SUNDAY	MONDAY	TUESDAY	WEDNESDAY	THURSDAY	FRIDAY	SATURDAY
27	28	29	30	1	2 Sukkot begins	3
4	5	6	7	8	9	10
11	12 Columbus Day (USA); Thanksgiving Day (CAN)	13	14	15	16	17
18	19	20	21	22	23	24
25	26	27	28	29	30	31 Halloween

CREATURE OF HABIT

Track new goals or habits and watch your progress every month!

HABIT	1	2	3	4	5	6	7	8	9	10	11	12	13	14	15	16	17	18	19	20	21	22	23	24	25	26	27	28	29	30	31

2020 SEPTEMBER/OCTOBER

MONDAY
28

TUESDAY
29

THE BEST WAY TO PREDICT
THE FUTURE IS TO CREATE IT.

WEDNESDAY
30

THURSDAY
1

CASH IN YOUR KARMA WITH A LITTLE BREAK.

FRIDAY
2

Sukkot begins

LIFE IS BETTER
IN PJ'S! RELAX!

SATURDAY
3

SUNDAY
4

DON'T FORGET:

THIS WEEK'S
HAPPY MOMENT:

OCTOBER 2020

S	M	T	W	T	F	S
				1	2	3
4	5	6	7	8	9	10
11	12	13	14	15	16	17
18	19	20	21	22	23	24
25	26	27	28	29	30	31

NOVEMBER 2020

S	M	T	W	T	F	S
1	2	3	4	5	6	7
8	9	10	11	12	13	14
15	16	17	18	19	20	21
22	23	24	25	26	27	28
29	30					

2020 OCTOBER

MONDAY
5

BE A WARRIOR, NOT A WORRIER.

TUESDAY
6

WEDNESDAY
7

THERE IS GOOD, AND YOU WILL FIND IT!

THURSDAY
8

PAT YOURSELF ON THE BACK FOR MAKING IT THROUGH ANOTHER WEEK!

FRIDAY
9

SATURDAY
10

CHOOSE PEOPLE WHO CHOOSE YOU.

SUNDAY
11

DON'T FORGET:

THIS WEEK'S HAPPY MOMENT:

OCTOBER 2020

S	M	T	W	T	F	S
				1	2	3
4	5	6	7	8	9	10
11	12	13	14	15	16	17
18	19	20	21	22	23	24
25	26	27	28	29	30	31

NOVEMBER 2020

S	M	T	W	T	F	S
1	2	3	4	5	6	7
8	9	10	11	12	13	14
15	16	17	18	19	20	21
22	23	24	25	26	27	28
29	30					

2020 **OCTOBER**

MONDAY
12

Columbus Day (USA); Thanksgiving Day (CAN)

TUESDAY
13

THE BEST VIEWS COME AFTER THE HARDEST CLIMBS.

WEDNESDAY
14

THURSDAY
15

BE YOURSELF. YOU NEVER KNOW WHO YOU'RE INSPIRING.

FRIDAY
16

NEVER STOP
LOOKING UP!

SATURDAY
17

SUNDAY
18

DON'T FORGET:

OCTOBER 2020

S	M	T	W	T	F	S
				1	2	3
4	5	6	7	8	9	10
11	12	13	14	15	16	17
18	19	20	21	22	23	24
25	26	27	28	29	30	31

NOVEMBER 2020

S	M	T	W	T	F	S
1	2	3	4	5	6	7
8	9	10	11	12	13	14
15	16	17	18	19	20	21
22	23	24	25	26	27	28
29	30					

THIS WEEK'S
HAPPY MOMENT:

2020 OCTOBER

MONDAY
19

TOO RAD TO BE SAD!

TUESDAY
20

WEDNESDAY
21

BE THE GAME CHANGER.

THURSDAY
22

YOU WILL BE OKAY EVEN IF SOME THINGS DON'T FALL INTO PLACE.

FRIDAY
23

SATURDAY
24

HERE'S A REMINDER TO BE EXTRA SWEET TO YOURSELF!

SUNDAY
25

DON'T FORGET:

THIS WEEK'S HAPPY MOMENT:

OCTOBER 2020

S	M	T	W	T	F	S
				1	2	3
4	5	6	7	8	9	10
11	12	13	14	15	16	17
18	19	20	21	22	23	24
25	26	27	28	29	30	31

NOVEMBER 2020

S	M	T	W	T	F	S
1	2	3	4	5	6	7
8	9	10	11	12	13	14
15	16	17	18	19	20	21
22	23	24	25	26	27	28
29	30					

2020 OCTOBER/NOVEMBER

MONDAY
26

TUESDAY
27

MAKE YOURSELF YOUR
#1 PRIORITY TODAY!

WEDNESDAY
28

THURSDAY
29

REMEMBER WHY YOU STARTED.

FRIDAY
30

YOU'RE SO
INCREDIBLE,
IT'S SCARY!

SATURDAY
31

Halloween

SUNDAY
1

Daylight Saving Time ends (USA, CAN)

DON'T FORGET:

OCTOBER 2020

S	M	T	W	T	F	S
				1	2	3
4	5	6	7	8	9	10
11	12	13	14	15	16	17
18	19	20	21	22	23	24
25	26	27	28	29	30	31

NOVEMBER 2020

S	M	T	W	T	F	S
1	2	3	4	5	6	7
8	9	10	11	12	13	14
15	16	17	18	19	20	21
22	23	24	25	26	27	28
29	30					

THIS WEEK'S
HAPPY MOMENT:

MONTHLY GOALS

NEW GOALS TO FOCUS ON

WHAT WORKED LAST MONTH

WHAT COULD BE BETTER

We are
ALL
in this
TOGETHER

NOVEMBER 2020

SUNDAY	MONDAY	TUESDAY	WEDNESDAY	THURSDAY	FRIDAY	SATURDAY
1 Daylight Saving Time ends (USA, CAN)	2	3 Election Day	4	5	6	7
8	9	10	11 Veterans Day (USA); Remembrance Day (CAN, UK)	12	13	14 Diwali begins
15	16	17	18	19	20	21
22	23	24	25	26 Thanksgiving Day	27	28
29	30 St. Andrew's Day (SCT)	1	2	3	4	5

CREATURE OF HABIT

Track new goals or habits and watch your progress every month!

HABIT	1	2	3	4	5	6	7	8	9	10	11	12	13	14	15	16	17	18	19	20	21	22	23	24	25	26	27	28	29	30	31

2020 **NOVEMBER**

MONDAY
2

NEW DAY. NEW START. LET'S DO THIS!

TUESDAY
3

Election Day

WEDNESDAY
4

YOU DESERVE CARE AND GENTLENESS, TOO.

THURSDAY
5

YOU CHANGE THE WORLD FOR THE BETTER EVERY SINGLE DAY.

FRIDAY 6

SATURDAY 7

IT'S SUNDAY! BE A LITTLE WILD.

SUNDAY 8

DON'T FORGET:

THIS WEEK'S HAPPY MOMENT:

NOVEMBER 2020

S	M	T	W	T	F	S
1	2	3	4	5	6	7
8	9	10	11	12	13	14
15	16	17	18	19	20	21
22	23	24	25	26	27	28
29	30					

DECEMBER 2020

S	M	T	W	T	F	S
		1	2	3	4	5
6	7	8	9	10	11	12
13	14	15	16	17	18	19
20	21	22	23	24	25	26
27	28	29	30	31		

2020 NOVEMBER

MONDAY
9

TUESDAY
10

MISTAKES ARE PROOF THAT YOU'RE TRYING.

WEDNESDAY
11

Veterans Day (USA); Remembrance Day (CAN, UK)

THURSDAY
12

TODAY IS YOUR DAY!

FRIDAY
13

IT'S KIND
OF FUN
TO DO THE
IMPOSSIBLE.

SATURDAY
14

Diwali begins

SUNDAY
15

DON'T FORGET:

THIS WEEK'S
HAPPY MOMENT:

NOVEMBER 2020

S	M	T	W	T	F	S
1	2	3	4	5	6	7
8	9	10	11	12	13	14
15	16	17	18	19	20	21
22	23	24	25	26	27	28
29	30					

DECEMBER 2020

S	M	T	W	T	F	S
		1	2	3	4	5
6	7	8	9	10	11	12
13	14	15	16	17	18	19
20	21	22	23	24	25	26
27	28	29	30	31		

2020 **NOVEMBER**

MONDAY
16

WRAP YOURSELF IN GRATITUDE
LIKE A WARM BLANKET!

TUESDAY
17

WEDNESDAY
18

IF THINGS ARE GETTING YOU DOWN,
CALL FOR BACKUP!
A FRIEND MAY BE ALL YOU NEED.

THURSDAY
19

THE ONLY DIFFERENCE BETWEEN DRAMA AND COMEDY IS PERSPECTIVE.

FRIDAY 20

SATURDAY 21

YOU ARE SERIOUSLY GREAT!

SUNDAY 22

DON'T FORGET:

THIS WEEK'S HAPPY MOMENT:

NOVEMBER 2020

S	M	T	W	T	F	S
1	2	3	4	5	6	7
8	9	10	11	12	13	14
15	16	17	18	19	20	21
22	23	24	25	26	27	28
29	30					

DECEMBER 2020

S	M	T	W	T	F	S
		1	2	3	4	5
6	7	8	9	10	11	12
13	14	15	16	17	18	19
20	21	22	23	24	25	26
27	28	29	30	31		

2020 NOVEMBER

MONDAY
23

TUESDAY
24

HOW CAN YOU SHOW UP FULLY IN YOUR LIFE?

WEDNESDAY
25

THURSDAY
26

JOY STARTS WITH A GRATEFUL HEART.

Thanksgiving Day

FRIDAY
27

GRIN AND
SHARE IT!

SATURDAY
28

SUNDAY
29

DON'T FORGET:

THIS WEEK'S
HAPPY MOMENT:

NOVEMBER 2020

S	M	T	W	T	F	S
1	2	3	4	5	6	7
8	9	10	11	12	13	14
15	16	17	18	19	20	21
22	23	24	25	26	27	28
29	30					

DECEMBER 2020

S	M	T	W	T	F	S
		1	2	3	4	5
6	7	8	9	10	11	12
13	14	15	16	17	18	19
20	21	22	23	24	25	26
27	28	29	30	31		

MONTHLY GOALS

NEW GOALS TO FOCUS ON

WHAT WORKED LAST MONTH

WHAT COULD BE BETTER

SELF LOVE IS YOUR SUPER POWER

DECEMBER 2020

SUNDAY	MONDAY	TUESDAY	WEDNESDAY	THURSDAY	FRIDAY	SATURDAY
29	30	1	2	3	4	5
6	7 Pearl Harbor Day	8	9	10 Hanukkah begins	11	12
13	14	15	16	17	18	19
20	21 Winter begins (Northern Hemisphere)	22	23	24 Christmas Eve	25 Christmas Day	26 Kwanzaa begins; Boxing Day (AUS, CAN, NZ, UK)
27	28	29	30	31 New Year's Eve	1	2

CREATURE OF HABIT

Track new goals or habits and watch your progress every month!

HABIT	1	2	3	4	5	6	7	8	9	10	11	12	13	14	15	16	17	18	19	20	21	22	23	24	25	26	27	28	29	30	31

2020 NOVEMBER/DECEMBER

MONDAY
30

WHAT SHOULD YOU DO TODAY?
SMILE. SMILE A LOT.

St. Andrew's Day (SCT)

TUESDAY
1

WEDNESDAY
2

YOU MAY NOT ALWAYS FEEL LIKE THE STAR YOU ARE,
BUT YOU KEEP SHINING ANYWAY!

THURSDAY
3

LIFE'S TOO SHORT TO NOT EXPRESS YOURSELF!

FRIDAY 4

SATURDAY 5

YOU ARE UNSTOPPABLE.

SUNDAY 6

DON'T FORGET:

THIS WEEK'S HAPPY MOMENT:

DECEMBER 2020

S	M	T	W	T	F	S
		1	2	3	4	5
6	7	8	9	10	11	12
13	14	15	16	17	18	19
20	21	22	23	24	25	26
27	28	29	30	31		

JANUARY 2021

S	M	T	W	T	F	S
					1	2
3	4	5	6	7	8	9
10	11	12	13	14	15	16
17	18	19	20	21	22	23
24/31	25	26	27	28	29	30

2020 DECEMBER

MONDAY
7

Pearl Harbor Day

TUESDAY
8

CALL SOMEONE YOU CARE ABOUT AND TELL THEM WHY YOU LOVE THEM!

WEDNESDAY
9

THURSDAY
10

DON'T LET THE UNKNOWN INTIMIDATE YOU.

Hanukkah begins

FRIDAY
11

NO STRUGGLE =
NO PROGRESS

SATURDAY
12

SUNDAY
13

DON'T FORGET:

THIS WEEK'S
HAPPY MOMENT:

DECEMBER 2020

S	M	T	W	T	F	S
		1	2	3	4	5
6	7	8	9	10	11	12
13	14	15	16	17	18	19
20	21	22	23	24	25	26
27	28	29	30	31		

JANUARY 2021

S	M	T	W	T	F	S
					1	2
3	4	5	6	7	8	9
10	11	12	13	14	15	16
17	18	19	20	21	22	23
24/31	25	26	27	28	29	30

2020 **DECEMBER**

MONDAY
14

DARE TO BE DIFFERENT!

TUESDAY
15

WEDNESDAY
16

DO MORE OF WHAT MAKES YOU HAPPY.

THURSDAY
17

IT'S THE MOST WONDERFUL TIME OF THE YEAR! CHERISH IT.

FRIDAY 18

SATURDAY 19

FRIENDS, HOT COCOA, AND HOLIDAY MOVIES. YOU KNOW WHAT TO DO!

SUNDAY 20

DON'T FORGET:

THIS WEEK'S HAPPY MOMENT:

DECEMBER 2020

S	M	T	W	T	F	S
		1	2	3	4	5
6	7	8	9	10	11	12
13	14	15	16	17	18	19
20	21	22	23	24	25	26
27	28	29	30	31		

JANUARY 2021

S	M	T	W	T	F	S
					1	2
3	4	5	6	7	8	9
10	11	12	13	14	15	16
17	18	19	20	21	22	23
24/31	25	26	27	28	29	30

2020 **DECEMBER**

MONDAY
21

Winter begins (Northern Hemisphere)

TUESDAY
22

STARS CAN'T SHINE WITHOUT DARKNESS.

WEDNESDAY
23

THURSDAY
24

BE MERRY AND BRIGHT!

Christmas Eve

FRIDAY
25

Christmas Day

BEAUTIFUL
MINDS
INSPIRE
OTHERS.

SATURDAY
26

Kwanzaa begins; Boxing Day (AUS, CAN, NZ, UK)

SUNDAY
27

DON'T FORGET:

DECEMBER 2020

S	M	T	W	T	F	S
		1	2	3	4	5
6	7	8	9	10	11	12
13	14	15	16	17	18	19
20	21	22	23	24	25	26
27	28	29	30	31		

JANUARY 2021

S	M	T	W	T	F	S
					1	2
3	4	5	6	7	8	9
10	11	12	13	14	15	16
17	18	19	20	21	22	23
24/31	25	26	27	28	29	30

THIS WEEK'S
HAPPY MOMENT:

2020/21 DECEMBER/JANUARY

MONDAY
28

YOU MAKE A DIFFERENCE IN THIS WORLD.

TUESDAY
29

WEDNESDAY
30

REMINISCE ABOUT HOW
WONDERFUL YOUR YEAR WAS.

THURSDAY
31

New Year's Eve

NEW YEAR'S RESOLUTION:
KEEP BEING AWESOME!

FRIDAY
1

New Year's Day

SATURDAY
2

Day after New Year's Day (NZ, SCT)

YOU ARE SO READY FOR THIS YEAR! BRING IT ON, 2021!

SUNDAY
3

DON'T FORGET:

THIS WEEK'S
HAPPY MOMENT:

DECEMBER 2020

S	M	T	W	T	F	S
		1	2	3	4	5
6	7	8	9	10	11	12
13	14	15	16	17	18	19
20	21	22	23	24	25	26
27	28	29	30	31		

JANUARY 2021

S	M	T	W	T	F	S
					1	2
3	4	5	6	7	8	9
10	11	12	13	14	15	16
17	18	19	20	21	22	23
24/31	25	26	27	28	29	30

MONTHLY GOALS

NEW GOALS TO FOCUS ON

WHAT WORKED LAST MONTH

WHAT COULD BE BETTER

YOU GOT THIS

JANUARY 2021

SUNDAY	MONDAY	TUESDAY	WEDNESDAY	THURSDAY	FRIDAY	SATURDAY
27	28	29	30	31	1 New Year's Day	2 Day after New Year's Day (NZ, SCT)
3	4	5	6	7	8	9
10	11	12	13	14	15	16
17	18 Martin Luther King Jr. Day	19	20	21	22	23
24/31	25	26 Australia Day (AUS)	27	28	29	30

CREATURE OF HABIT

Track new goals or habits
and watch your progress
every month!

HABIT	1	2	3	4	5	6	7	8	9	10	11	12	13	14	15	16	17	18	19	20	21	22	23	24	25	26	27	28	29	30	31

2021 JANUARY

MONDAY
4

TUESDAY
5

HOW BEAUTIFULLY YOU'VE
GROWN SINCE LAST YEAR!

WEDNESDAY
6

THURSDAY
7

INHALE THE FUTURE. EXHALE THE PAST.

FRIDAY
8

YOU GO AHEAD
AND DO YOU.
YOU'RE A
NATURAL AT IT.

SATURDAY
9

SUNDAY
10

DON'T FORGET:

JANUARY 2021

S	M	T	W	T	F	S
					1	2
3	4	5	6	7	8	9
10	11	12	13	14	15	16
17	18	19	20	21	22	23
24/31	25	26	27	28	29	30

FEBRUARY 2021

S	M	T	W	T	F	S
	1	2	3	4	5	6
7	8	9	10	11	12	13
14	15	16	17	18	19	20
21	22	23	24	25	26	27
28						

THIS WEEK'S
HAPPY MOMENT:

2021 JANUARY

MONDAY
11

TAKE TIME TO MAKE YOUR SOUL HAPPY.

TUESDAY
12

WEDNESDAY
13

DON'T FORGET TO GO SHARE SOME LOVE.

THURSDAY
14

LET PEOPLE SEE THE REAL, IMPERFECT, WEIRD, BEAUTIFUL, MAGICAL PERSON THAT YOU ARE.

FRIDAY
15

SATURDAY
16

GO MAKE SOMEONE'S DAY! HOW'D IT FEEL?

SUNDAY
17

DON'T FORGET:

THIS WEEK'S HAPPY MOMENT:

JANUARY 2021

S	M	T	W	T	F	S
					1	2
3	4	5	6	7	8	9
10	11	12	13	14	15	16
17	18	19	20	21	22	23
24/31	25	26	27	28	29	30

FEBRUARY 2021

S	M	T	W	T	F	S
	1	2	3	4	5	6
7	8	9	10	11	12	13
14	15	16	17	18	19	20
21	22	23	24	25	26	27
28						

2021 JANUARY

MONDAY
18

Martin Luther King Jr. Day

TUESDAY
19

DO YOU HAVE ANY IDEA
HOW STRONG YOU ARE?

WEDNESDAY
20

THURSDAY
21

SHAKE AWAY THE WINTER BLUES
WITH A DANCE PARTY!

FRIDAY
22

SATURDAY
23

LOOK IN
THE MIRROR
AND REMIND
YOURSELF
HOW
BRILLIANT
YOU ARE.

SUNDAY
24

DON'T FORGET:

THIS WEEK'S
HAPPY MOMENT:

JANUARY 2021

S	M	T	W	T	F	S
					1	2
3	4	5	6	7	8	9
10	11	12	13	14	15	16
17	18	19	20	21	22	23
24/31	25	26	27	28	29	30

FEBRUARY 2021

S	M	T	W	T	F	S
	1	2	3	4	5	6
7	8	9	10	11	12	13
14	15	16	17	18	19	20
21	22	23	24	25	26	27
28						

2021 JANUARY

MONDAY
25

EXCELLENCE IS A HABIT. KEEP GOING!

TUESDAY
26

Australia Day (AUS)

WEDNESDAY
27

YOUR SMILE IS STUPENDOUS! SHOW IT OFF.

THURSDAY
28

ADD A LITTLE EXTRA TO YOUR ORDINARY!

FRIDAY 29

SATURDAY 30

CUDDLING RELEASES STRESS AND BOOSTS HAPPINESS. YOU KNOW WHAT TO DO!

SUNDAY 31

DON'T FORGET:

THIS WEEK'S HAPPY MOMENT:

JANUARY 2021

S	M	T	W	T	F	S
					1	2
3	4	5	6	7	8	9
10	11	12	13	14	15	16
17	18	19	20	21	22	23
24/31	25	26	27	28	29	30

FEBRUARY 2021

S	M	T	W	T	F	S
	1	2	3	4	5	6
7	8	9	10	11	12	13
14	15	16	17	18	19	20
21	22	23	24	25	26	27
28						

MONTHLY GOALS

NEW GOALS TO FOCUS ON

WHAT WORKED LAST MONTH

WHAT COULD BE BETTER

JUST ENJOY WHERE YOU ARE NOW

FEBRUARY 2021

SUNDAY	MONDAY	TUESDAY	WEDNESDAY	THURSDAY	FRIDAY	SATURDAY
31	1	2 Groundhog Day	3	4	5	6 Waitangi Day (NZ)
7	8	9	10	11	12 Abraham Lincoln's Birthday; Chinese New Year	13
14 Valentine's Day	15 Presidents' Day	16	17 Ash Wednesday (Lent begins)	18	19	20
21	22	23	24	25 Purim begins	26	27
28	1	2	3	4	5	6

CREATURE OF HABIT

Track new goals or habits and watch your progress every month!

HABIT	1	2	3	4	5	6	7	8	9	10	11	12	13	14	15	16	17	18	19	20	21	22	23	24	25	26	27	28	29	30	31

2021 FEBRUARY

MONDAY
1

TUESDAY
2

A GROUNDHOG MAY DECIDE THE WEATHER, BUT YOU DECIDE HOW YOUR DAY GOES!

Groundhog Day

WEDNESDAY
3

THURSDAY
4

THE BEST IS YET TO COME.

FRIDAY
5

SATURDAY
6

GIVE
YOURSELF A
HIGH-FIVE.
YOU'RE
DOING
GREAT!

Waitangi Day (NZ)

SUNDAY
7

DON'T FORGET:

THIS WEEK'S
HAPPY MOMENT:

FEBRUARY 2021

S	M	T	W	T	F	S
	1	2	3	4	5	6
7	8	9	10	11	12	13
14	15	16	17	18	19	20
21	22	23	24	25	26	27
28						

MARCH 2021

S	M	T	W	T	F	S
	1	2	3	4	5	6
7	8	9	10	11	12	13
14	15	16	17	18	19	20
21	22	23	24	25	26	27
28	29	30	31			

2021 FEBRUARY

MONDAY
8

TRUST YOURSELF COMPLETELY.

TUESDAY
9

WEDNESDAY
10

YOU ARE WORTHY OF
GREAT NEW BEGINNINGS.

THURSDAY
11

WEEKEND RELAXATION, HERE YOU COME!

FRIDAY 12

Abraham Lincoln's Birthday; Chinese New Year

SATURDAY 13

BE YOUR OWN VALENTINE AND LOVE YOURSELF.

SUNDAY 14

Valentine's Day

DON'T FORGET:

THIS WEEK'S HAPPY MOMENT:

FEBRUARY 2021

S	M	T	W	T	F	S
	1	2	3	4	5	6
7	8	9	10	11	12	13
14	15	16	17	18	19	20
21	22	23	24	25	26	27
28						

MARCH 2021

S	M	T	W	T	F	S
	1	2	3	4	5	6
7	8	9	10	11	12	13
14	15	16	17	18	19	20
21	22	23	24	25	26	27
28	29	30	31			

2021 **FEBRUARY**

MONDAY
15

Presidents' Day

TUESDAY
16

BREAK OUT OF YOUR COMFORT ZONE!
YOU'LL BE GLAD YOU DID.

WEDNESDAY
17

Ash Wednesday (Lent begins)

THURSDAY
18

SMILE BIG AND STAND TALL.

FRIDAY
19

SATURDAY
20

DID YOU
KNOW
YOU'RE
DOING
INCREDIBLE
THINGS?

SUNDAY
21

DON'T FORGET:

THIS WEEK'S
HAPPY MOMENT:

FEBRUARY 2021

S	M	T	W	T	F	S
	1	2	3	4	5	6
7	8	9	10	11	12	13
14	15	16	17	18	19	20
21	22	23	24	25	26	27
28						

MARCH 2021

S	M	T	W	T	F	S
	1	2	3	4	5	6
7	8	9	10	11	12	13
14	15	16	17	18	19	20
21	22	23	24	25	26	27
28	29	30	31			

2021 **FEBRUARY**

MONDAY
22

YOU CAN'T STOP CHANGE FROM HAPPENING, SO HOW WILL YOU EVOLVE?

TUESDAY
23

WEDNESDAY
24

MAKE YOUR OWN KIND OF MUSIC!

THURSDAY
25

Purim begins

YOU ARE THE AUTHOR OF YOUR STORY, AND IT'S GOING TO BE A REAL PAGE-TURNER!

FRIDAY 26

SATURDAY 27

SUNDAY 28

SEEMS LIKE THE PERFECT DAY FOR A QUICK NAP. RELAX!

DON'T FORGET:

THIS WEEK'S HAPPY MOMENT:

FEBRUARY 2021

S	M	T	W	T	F	S
	1	2	3	4	5	6
7	8	9	10	11	12	13
14	15	16	17	18	19	20
21	22	23	24	25	26	27
28						

MARCH 2021

S	M	T	W	T	F	S
	1	2	3	4	5	6
7	8	9	10	11	12	13
14	15	16	17	18	19	20
21	22	23	24	25	26	27
28	29	30	31			

MONTHLY GOALS

NEW GOALS TO FOCUS ON

WHAT WORKED LAST MONTH

WHAT COULD BE BETTER

DON'T WAIT...
the TIME will never
be just RIGHT

MARCH 2021

SUNDAY	MONDAY	TUESDAY	WEDNESDAY	THURSDAY	FRIDAY	SATURDAY
28	1	2	3	4	5	6
7	8 International Women's Day; Public Holiday (AUS: ACT, SA, TAS, VIC)	9	10	11	12	13
14 Daylight Saving Time begins (USA, CAN); Mothering Sunday (UK)	15	16	17 St. Patrick's Day	18	19	20 Spring begins (Northern Hemisphere)
21	22	23	24	25	26	27 Passover begins
28 Palm Sunday	29	30	31	1	2	3

CREATURE OF HABIT

Track new goals or habits and watch your progress every month!

HABIT	1	2	3	4	5	6	7	8	9	10	11	12	13	14	15	16	17	18	19	20	21	22	23	24	25	26	27	28	29	30	31

2021 **MARCH**

MONDAY
1

TUESDAY
2

THIS WEEK'S TO-DO LIST: STOP STRESSING. BE FABULOUS. REPEAT.

WEDNESDAY
3

THURSDAY
4

BETTER AN "OOPS" THAN A "WHAT IF?"

FRIDAY
5

SATURDAY
6

WHEN DID YOU LAST GAZE AT THE STARS? THEY'RE SHINING DOWN ON YOU.

SUNDAY
7

DON'T FORGET:

MARCH 2021

S	M	T	W	T	F	S
	1	2	3	4	5	6
7	8	9	10	11	12	13
14	15	16	17	18	19	20
21	22	23	24	25	26	27
28	29	30	31			

APRIL 2021

S	M	T	W	T	F	S
				1	2	3
4	5	6	7	8	9	10
11	12	13	14	15	16	17
18	19	20	21	22	23	24
25	26	27	28	29	30	

THIS WEEK'S HAPPY MOMENT:

2021 **MARCH**

MONDAY
8

WE RISE BY LIFTING EACH OTHER UP.

International Women's Day; Public Holiday (AUS: ACT, SA, TAS, VIC)

TUESDAY
9

WEDNESDAY
10

IT'S A GOOD DAY TO SPOIL YOURSELF.
BUBBLE BATH, ANYONE?

THURSDAY
11

BE COOL AND STAY CALM.

FRIDAY
12

SATURDAY
13

SUNDAY
14

SPRING FORWARD WITH YOUR CLOCK AND GET PUMPED FOR THE WEEK AHEAD!

Daylight Saving Time begins (USA, CAN); Mothering Sunday (UK)

DON'T FORGET:

THIS WEEK'S HAPPY MOMENT:

MARCH 2021

S	M	T	W	T	F	S
	1	2	3	4	5	6
7	8	9	10	11	12	13
14	15	16	17	18	19	20
21	22	23	24	25	26	27
28	29	30	31			

APRIL 2021

S	M	T	W	T	F	S
				1	2	3
4	5	6	7	8	9	10
11	12	13	14	15	16	17
18	19	20	21	22	23	24
25	26	27	28	29	30	

2021 MARCH

MONDAY
15

TUESDAY
16

TAKE TIME TO REFLECT TODAY. YOU'RE MARVELOUS AND YOU SHOULD OWN IT!

WEDNESDAY
17

St. Patrick's Day

THURSDAY
18

IT MUST FEEL PRETTY LUCKY TO BE YOU!

FRIDAY
19

SATURDAY
20

SPRING IS HERE! PUT A LITTLE MORE BOUNCE IN YOUR STEP!

Spring begins (Northern Hemisphere)

SUNDAY
21

DON'T FORGET:

THIS WEEK'S HAPPY MOMENT:

MARCH 2021

S	M	T	W	T	F	S
	1	2	3	4	5	6
7	8	9	10	11	12	13
14	15	16	17	18	19	20
21	22	23	24	25	26	27
28	29	30	31			

APRIL 2021

S	M	T	W	T	F	S
				1	2	3
4	5	6	7	8	9	10
11	12	13	14	15	16	17
18	19	20	21	22	23	24
25	26	27	28	29	30	

2021 **MARCH**

MONDAY
22

YOU CAN'T ALWAYS CONTROL WHAT THOUGHTS POP INTO YOUR HEAD, BUT YOU CAN DECIDE WHAT TO DWELL ON.

TUESDAY
23

WEDNESDAY
24

HAPPINESS ISN'T SOMETHING YOU PURSUE. IT'S SOMETHING YOU DO!

THURSDAY
25

THE GRASS IS GREENER
WHEREVER YOU ARE!

FRIDAY 26

SATURDAY 27

Passover begins

NOTHING IN NATURE BLOOMS ALL YEAR.

SUNDAY 28

Palm Sunday

DON'T FORGET:

THIS WEEK'S HAPPY MOMENT:

MARCH 2021

S	M	T	W	T	F	S
	1	2	3	4	5	6
7	8	9	10	11	12	13
14	15	16	17	18	19	20
21	22	23	24	25	26	27
28	29	30	31			

APRIL 2021

S	M	T	W	T	F	S
				1	2	3
4	5	6	7	8	9	10
11	12	13	14	15	16	17
18	19	20	21	22	23	24
25	26	27	28	29	30	

MONTHLY GOALS

NEW GOALS TO FOCUS ON

WHAT WORKED LAST MONTH

WHAT COULD BE BETTER

Bloom
WHERE YOU ARE
planted

APRIL 2021

SUNDAY	MONDAY	TUESDAY	WEDNESDAY	THURSDAY	FRIDAY	SATURDAY
28	29	30	31	1 April Fools' Day	2 Good Friday	3
4 Easter	5 Easter Monday (AUS, CAN, NZ, UK except SCT)	6	7	8	9	10
11	12 Ramadan begins	13	14	15 Tax Day	16	17
18	19	20	21	22 Earth Day	23	24
25 Anzac Day (AUS, NZ)	26	27	28 Workers' Memorial Day (UK)	29	30	1

CREATURE OF HABIT

Track new goals or habits
and watch your progress
every month!

HABIT	1	2	3	4	5	6	7	8	9	10	11	12	13	14	15	16	17	18	19	20	21	22	23	24	25	26	27	28	29	30	31

2021 MARCH/APRIL

MONDAY
29

TUESDAY
30

LET SOMEONE UNDER
YOUR UMBRELLA THIS WEEK.

WEDNESDAY
31

THURSDAY
1

DON'T BE AFRAID TO GET SILLY SOMETIMES!

April Fools' Day

FRIDAY
2

Good Friday

KEEP ON
KEEPING ON.

SATURDAY
3

SUNDAY
4

Easter

DON'T FORGET:

THIS WEEK'S
HAPPY MOMENT:

APRIL 2021

S	M	T	W	T	F	S
				1	2	3
4	5	6	7	8	9	10
11	12	13	14	15	16	17
18	19	20	21	22	23	24
25	26	27	28	29	30	

MAY 2021

S	M	T	W	T	F	S
						1
2	3	4	5	6	7	8
9	10	11	12	13	14	15
16	17	18	19	20	21	22
23/30	24/31	25	26	27	28	29

2021 **APRIL**

MONDAY
5

IT'S OKAY TO LET GO SOMETIMES.

Easter Monday (AUS, CAN, NZ, UK except SCT)

TUESDAY
6

WEDNESDAY
7

EVERY DAY IS A FRESH START.

THURSDAY
8

LIGHT TOMORROW WITH TODAY.

FRIDAY
9

SATURDAY
10

ONLY YOU
CAN BUILD
A LIFE YOU
LOVE.

SUNDAY
11

DON'T FORGET:

THIS WEEK'S
HAPPY MOMENT:

APRIL 2021

S	M	T	W	T	F	S
				1	2	3
4	5	6	7	8	9	10
11	12	13	14	15	16	17
18	19	20	21	22	23	24
25	26	27	28	29	30	

MAY 2021

S	M	T	W	T	F	S
						1
2	3	4	5	6	7	8
9	10	11	12	13	14	15
16	17	18	19	20	21	22
23/30	24/31	25	26	27	28	29

2021 **APRIL**

MONDAY
12

Ramadan begins

TUESDAY
13

NOTHING CAN RAIN ON YOUR PARADE TODAY!

WEDNESDAY
14

THURSDAY
15

BE THE BEST *YOU* YOU CAN BE.

Tax Day

FRIDAY
16

SATURDAY
17

HAPPINESS
IS A DISH
BEST SHARED
WITH
OTHERS.

SUNDAY
18

DON'T FORGET:

THIS WEEK'S
HAPPY MOMENT:

APRIL 2021

S	M	T	W	T	F	S
				1	2	3
4	5	6	7	8	9	10
11	12	13	14	15	16	17
18	19	20	21	22	23	24
25	26	27	28	29	30	

MAY 2021

S	M	T	W	T	F	S
						1
2	3	4	5	6	7	8
9	10	11	12	13	14	15
16	17	18	19	20	21	22
23/30	24/31	25	26	27	28	29

2021 **APRIL**

MONDAY
19

MONDAYS ARE NO MATCH FOR YOU!

TUESDAY
20

WEDNESDAY
21

SHOWER YOUR ATTENTION ON SELF-LOVE AND DREAMS, NOT FEARS OR INSECURITIES.

THURSDAY
22

Earth Day

WHAT A WEEK! TAKE A WELL-DESERVED BREAK.

FRIDAY 23

SATURDAY 24

SUNDAY 25

YOU ARE MIND-BLOWINGLY MAGNIFICENT!

Anzac Day (AUS, NZ)

DON'T FORGET:

THIS WEEK'S HAPPY MOMENT:

APRIL 2021

S	M	T	W	T	F	S
				1	2	3
4	5	6	7	8	9	10
11	12	13	14	15	16	17
18	19	20	21	22	23	24
25	26	27	28	29	30	

MAY 2021

S	M	T	W	T	F	S
						1
2	3	4	5	6	7	8
9	10	11	12	13	14	15
16	17	18	19	20	21	22
23/30	24/31	25	26	27	28	29

MONDAY
26

TUESDAY
27

YOU ARE NOT WHAT HAPPENS TO YOU,
BUT WHAT YOU CHOOSE TO BECOME.

WEDNESDAY
28

Workers' Memorial Day (UK)

THURSDAY
29

MAKE AN EFFORT TO FEEL
PROUD OF YOURSELF TODAY.

FRIDAY
30

REMIND
YOURSELF
HOW
AWESOME
YOU ARE!

SATURDAY
1

SUNDAY
2

DON'T FORGET:

THIS WEEK'S
HAPPY MOMENT:

APRIL 2021

S	M	T	W	T	F	S
				1	2	3
4	5	6	7	8	9	10
11	12	13	14	15	16	17
18	19	20	21	22	23	24
25	26	27	28	29	30	

MAY 2021

S	M	T	W	T	F	S
						1
2	3	4	5	6	7	8
9	10	11	12	13	14	15
16	17	18	19	20	21	22
23/30	24/31	25	26	27	28	29

MONTHLY GOALS

NEW GOALS TO FOCUS ON

WHAT WORKED LAST MONTH

WHAT COULD BE BETTER

Believe you can AND YOU'RE HALFWAY there

MAY 2021

SUNDAY	MONDAY	TUESDAY	WEDNESDAY	THURSDAY	FRIDAY	SATURDAY
25	26	27	28	29	30	1
2	3	4	5 Cinco de Mayo	6	7	8
9 Mother's Day (USA, AUS, CAN, NZ)	10	11	12 Eid al-Fitr begins	13	14	15 Armed Forces Day
16 Shavuot begins	17	18	19	20	21	22
23/30	24/31 Victoria Day (24th: CAN) Memorial Day (31st USA); Spring Bank Holiday (31st: UK)	25	26	27	28	29

CREATURE OF HABIT

Track new goals or habits and watch your progress every month!

HABIT	1	2	3	4	5	6	7	8	9	10	11	12	13	14	15	16	17	18	19	20	21	22	23	24	25	26	27	28	29	30	31

MONDAY
3

BRIGHTEN UP YOUR MONDAY BY BUYING YOURSELF SOME FLOWERS!

TUESDAY
4

WEDNESDAY
5

CARPE THAT DIEM!

Cinco de Mayo

THURSDAY
6

GROW THROUGH WHAT YOU GO THROUGH.

FRIDAY 7

SATURDAY 8

SUNDAY 9

ONE SMALL ACT OF KINDNESS CAN CHANGE THE WORLD.

Mother's Day (USA, AUS, CAN, NZ)

DON'T FORGET:

THIS WEEK'S HAPPY MOMENT:

MAY 2021

S	M	T	W	T	F	S
						1
2	3	4	5	6	7	8
9	10	11	12	13	14	15
16	17	18	19	20	21	22
23/30	24/31	25	26	27	28	29

JUNE 2021

S	M	T	W	T	F	S
		1	2	3	4	5
6	7	8	9	10	11	12
13	14	15	16	17	18	19
20	21	22	23	24	25	26
27	28	29	30			

2021 MAY

MONDAY
10

TUESDAY
11

START YOUR DAY WITH
A DANCE PARTY AND GROOVE!

WEDNESDAY
12

Eid al-Fitr begins

THURSDAY
13

JOURNEYS WON'T ALWAYS BE PERFECT,
BUT THEY WILL TAKE YOU PLACES.

FRIDAY 14

GET TOTALLY ABSORBED IN SOMETHING YOU LOVE THIS WEEKEND.

SATURDAY 15

Armed Forces Day

SUNDAY 16

Shavuot begins

DON'T FORGET:

THIS WEEK'S HAPPY MOMENT:

MAY 2021

S	M	T	W	T	F	S
						1
2	3	4	5	6	7	8
9	10	11	12	13	14	15
16	17	18	19	20	21	22
23/30	24/31	25	26	27	28	29

JUNE 2021

S	M	T	W	T	F	S
		1	2	3	4	5
6	7	8	9	10	11	12
13	14	15	16	17	18	19
20	21	22	23	24	25	26
27	28	29	30			

2021 MAY

MONDAY
17

SPICE UP YOUR LIFE AND TRY SOMETHING NEW. IT MAY SURPRISE YOU!

TUESDAY
18

WEDNESDAY
19

YOU'RE THE UNDISPUTED WORLD CHAMPION OF BEING YOU!

THURSDAY
20

IF YOU MAKE OTHERS HAPPY, YOUR OWN HAPPINESS MAY WORK ITSELF OUT.

FRIDAY 21

SATURDAY 22

SUNDAY 23

TAKE EVERY CHANCE YOU CAN TO CONNECT WITH YOUR ROOTS.

DON'T FORGET:

THIS WEEK'S HAPPY MOMENT:

MAY 2021

S	M	T	W	T	F	S
						1
2	3	4	5	6	7	8
9	10	11	12	13	14	15
16	17	18	19	20	21	22
23/30	24/31	25	26	27	28	29

JUNE 2021

S	M	T	W	T	F	S
		1	2	3	4	5
6	7	8	9	10	11	12
13	14	15	16	17	18	19
20	21	22	23	24	25	26
27	28	29	30			

2021 MAY

MONDAY
24

Victoria Day (CAN)

TUESDAY
25

CHERISH THE SIMPLE THINGS. JOY CAN HIDE IN THE MOST OBVIOUS PLACES!

WEDNESDAY
26

THURSDAY
27

YOU'VE GOT THIS DAY! DESIGN IT HOW YOU WANT IT.

FRIDAY 28

SATURDAY 29

TAKE YOURSELF OUT TO LUNCH. YOU EARNED IT!

SUNDAY 30

DON'T FORGET:

THIS WEEK'S HAPPY MOMENT:

MAY 2021

S	M	T	W	T	F	S
						1
2	3	4	5	6	7	8
9	10	11	12	13	14	15
16	17	18	19	20	21	22
23/30	24/31	25	26	27	28	29

JUNE 2021

S	M	T	W	T	F	S
		1	2	3	4	5
6	7	8	9	10	11	12
13	14	15	16	17	18	19
20	21	22	23	24	25	26
27	28	29	30			

MONTHLY GOALS

NEW GOALS TO FOCUS ON

WHAT WORKED LAST MONTH

WHAT COULD BE BETTER

YOU
DESERVE
a BREAK

JUNE 2021

SUNDAY	MONDAY	TUESDAY	WEDNESDAY	THURSDAY	FRIDAY	SATURDAY
30	31	1	2	3	4	5
6	7	8	9	10	11	12
13	14 Flag Day	15	16	17	18	19
20 Father's Day (USA, CAN, UK); Summer begins (Northern Hemisphere)	21	22	23	24	25	26
27	28	29	30	1	2	3

CREATURE OF HABIT

Track new goals or habits and watch your progress every month!

HABIT	1	2	3	4	5	6	7	8	9	10	11	12	13	14	15	16	17	18	19	20	21	22	23	24	25	26	27	28	29	30	31

2021 **MAY/JUNE**

MONDAY
31

FLING AROUND JOY LIKE CONFETTI!

Memorial Day (USA); Spring Bank Holiday (UK)

TUESDAY
1

WEDNESDAY
2

CREATE YOUR OWN SUNSHINE.

THURSDAY
3

YOU WORK ON PURPOSE. DREAM ON PURPOSE. CHOOSE JOY ON PURPOSE!

FRIDAY
4

SATURDAY
5

STAY FLEXIBLE AND LEARN FROM YOUR SURROUNDINGS!

SUNDAY
6

DON'T FORGET:

THIS WEEK'S HAPPY MOMENT:

JUNE 2021

S	M	T	W	T	F	S
		1	2	3	4	5
6	7	8	9	10	11	12
13	14	15	16	17	18	19
20	21	22	23	24	25	26
27	28	29	30			

JULY 2021

S	M	T	W	T	F	S
				1	2	3
4	5	6	7	8	9	10
11	12	13	14	15	16	17
18	19	20	21	22	23	24
25	26	27	28	29	30	31

2021 JUNE

MONDAY
7

TUESDAY
8

THE SUN WILL ALWAYS RISE.

WEDNESDAY
9

THURSDAY
10

STAY GOLDEN.

FRIDAY
11

BELIEVE IN
YOURSELF.

SATURDAY
12

SUNDAY
13

DON'T FORGET:

THIS WEEK'S
HAPPY MOMENT:

JUNE 2021

S	M	T	W	T	F	S
		1	2	3	4	5
6	7	8	9	10	11	12
13	14	15	16	17	18	19
20	21	22	23	24	25	26
27	28	29	30			

JULY 2021

S	M	T	W	T	F	S
				1	2	3
4	5	6	7	8	9	10
11	12	13	14	15	16	17
18	19	20	21	22	23	24
25	26	27	28	29	30	31

2021 JUNE

MONDAY
14

THE DEEPEST OF FRIENDSHIPS OFTEN
BEGIN WITH JUST A SIMPLE SMILE.

Flag Day

TUESDAY
15

WEDNESDAY
16

BE SPONTANEOUS! WHERE'S YOUR
PLAYFUL SIDE TODAY?

THURSDAY
17

POSITIVE THOUGHTS CAN WILL YOUR DAY INTO BEING A GOOD ONE.

FRIDAY 18

SATURDAY 19

SUNDAY 20

THIS IS THE SUMMER OF YOU! MAKE THE MOST OF IT.

Father's Day (USA, CAN, UK); Summer begins (Northern Hemisphere)

DON'T FORGET:

THIS WEEK'S HAPPY MOMENT:

JUNE 2021

S	M	T	W	T	F	S
		1	2	3	4	5
6	7	8	9	10	11	12
13	14	15	16	17	18	19
20	21	22	23	24	25	26
27	28	29	30			

JULY 2021

S	M	T	W	T	F	S
				1	2	3
4	5	6	7	8	9	10
11	12	13	14	15	16	17
18	19	20	21	22	23	24
25	26	27	28	29	30	31

2021 **JUNE**

MONDAY
21

TUESDAY
22

BE A FLAMINGO IN A FLOCK OF PIGEONS.

WEDNESDAY
23

THURSDAY
24

DO SOMETHING TODAY THAT WOULD MAKE
YOUR EIGHT-YEAR-OLD SELF PROUD!

FRIDAY
25

SUNSHINE
MAKES YOU
HAPPIER.
SOAK UP
THOSE
RAYS THIS
WEEKEND!

SATURDAY
26

SUNDAY
27

DON'T FORGET:

JUNE 2021

S	M	T	W	T	F	S
		1	2	3	4	5
6	7	8	9	10	11	12
13	14	15	16	17	18	19
20	21	22	23	24	25	26
27	28	29	30			

JULY 2021

S	M	T	W	T	F	S
				1	2	3
4	5	6	7	8	9	10
11	12	13	14	15	16	17
18	19	20	21	22	23	24
25	26	27	28	29	30	31

THIS WEEK'S
HAPPY MOMENT:

MONTHLY GOALS

NEW GOALS TO FOCUS ON

WHAT WORKED LAST MONTH

WHAT COULD BE BETTER

DON'T TAKE
LIFE TOO
SERIOUSLY

JULY 2021

SUNDAY	MONDAY	TUESDAY	WEDNESDAY	THURSDAY	FRIDAY	SATURDAY
27	28	29	30	1 Canada Day (CAN)	2	3
4 Independence Day	5	6	7	8	9	10
11	12 Orangemen's Day—Battle of the Boyne (NIR)	13	14	15	16	17
18	19 Eid al-Adha begins	20	21	22	23	24
25	26	27	28	29	30	31

CREATURE OF HABIT

Track new goals or habits and watch your progress every month!

HABIT	1	2	3	4	5	6	7	8	9	10	11	12	13	14	15	16	17	18	19	20	21	22	23	24	25	26	27	28	29	30	31

2021 JUNE/JULY

MONDAY
28

NOTICE WHEN YOU'RE THE HAPPIEST.
RINSE AND REPEAT!

TUESDAY
29

WEDNESDAY
30

EVERYONE HAS TO BE THEIR OWN
SUPERHERO NOW AND THEN.

THURSDAY
1

Canada Day (CAN)

THE LIGHT YOU SEE IN OTHERS SHINES IN YOU TOO.

FRIDAY
2

SATURDAY
3

WE ALL KNOW YOU'RE THE REAL FIREWORK HERE!

SUNDAY
4

Independence Day

DON'T FORGET:

THIS WEEK'S HAPPY MOMENT:

JULY 2021

S	M	T	W	T	F	S
				1	2	3
4	5	6	7	8	9	10
11	12	13	14	15	16	17
18	19	20	21	22	23	24
25	26	27	28	29	30	31

AUGUST 2021

S	M	T	W	T	F	S
1	2	3	4	5	6	7
8	9	10	11	12	13	14
15	16	17	18	19	20	21
22	23	24	25	26	27	28
29	30	31				

2021 **JULY**

MONDAY
5

TUESDAY
6

WHOSE EYES LIGHT UP WHEN THEY SEE YOU? SURROUND YOURSELF WITH THOSE PEOPLE.

WEDNESDAY
7

THURSDAY
8

CHOOSE TO BE HAPPY TODAY.

FRIDAY
9

DO SOMETHING CREATIVE THIS WEEKEND. IT'LL REJUVENATE YOUR MIND.

SATURDAY
10

SUNDAY
11

DON'T FORGET:

THIS WEEK'S HAPPY MOMENT:

JULY 2021

S	M	T	W	T	F	S
				1	2	3
4	5	6	7	8	9	10
11	12	13	14	15	16	17
18	19	20	21	22	23	24
25	26	27	28	29	30	31

AUGUST 2021

S	M	T	W	T	F	S
1	2	3	4	5	6	7
8	9	10	11	12	13	14
15	16	17	18	19	20	21
22	23	24	25	26	27	28
29	30	31				

MONDAY
12

THERE IS NO ANGRY WAY TO SAY THE WORD "BUBBLES." TRY IT!

Orangemen's Day—Battle of the Boyne (NIR)

TUESDAY
13

WEDNESDAY
14

BE HAPPY FOR THIS MOMENT. THIS MOMENT IS YOUR LIFE.

THURSDAY
15

PHEW, WHAT A WEEK. BUT YOU MADE IT, AND THAT'S A WIN!

FRIDAY
16

SATURDAY
17

ALWAYS DANCE TO YOUR OWN RHYTHM!

SUNDAY
18

DON'T FORGET:

JULY 2021

S	M	T	W	T	F	S
				1	2	3
4	5	6	7	8	9	10
11	12	13	14	15	16	17
18	19	20	21	22	23	24
25	26	27	28	29	30	31

AUGUST 2021

S	M	T	W	T	F	S
1	2	3	4	5	6	7
8	9	10	11	12	13	14
15	16	17	18	19	20	21
22	23	24	25	26	27	28
29	30	31				

THIS WEEK'S HAPPY MOMENT:

MONDAY
19

Eid al-Adha begins

TUESDAY
20

GREAT THINGS ARE JUST
AROUND THE CORNER!

WEDNESDAY
21

THURSDAY
22

JOY COMES IN WAVES.
IT WILL ALWAYS FIND YOU AGAIN.

FRIDAY
23

SATURDAY
24

YOU'VE BEEN AWARDED A WEEKEND OF NO STRESS! KICK UP YOUR FEET AND CHILL.

SUNDAY
25

DON'T FORGET:

THIS WEEK'S HAPPY MOMENT:

JULY 2021

S	M	T	W	T	F	S
				1	2	3
4	5	6	7	8	9	10
11	12	13	14	15	16	17
18	19	20	21	22	23	24
25	26	27	28	29	30	31

AUGUST 2021

S	M	T	W	T	F	S
1	2	3	4	5	6	7
8	9	10	11	12	13	14
15	16	17	18	19	20	21
22	23	24	25	26	27	28
29	30	31				

MONDAY
26

WE ALL GROW AT DIFFERENT RATES,
AND THAT'S OKAY!

TUESDAY
27

WEDNESDAY
28

EVERYTHING STARTS WITH A DREAM.

THURSDAY
29

JUST BREATHE.

FRIDAY
30

SATURDAY
31

SMILE SO BRIGHT YOU HAVE TO WEAR SHADES!

SUNDAY
1

DON'T FORGET:

THIS WEEK'S HAPPY MOMENT:

JULY 2021

S	M	T	W	T	F	S
				1	2	3
4	5	6	7	8	9	10
11	12	13	14	15	16	17
18	19	20	21	22	23	24
25	26	27	28	29	30	31

AUGUST 2021

S	M	T	W	T	F	S
1	2	3	4	5	6	7
8	9	10	11	12	13	14
15	16	17	18	19	20	21
22	23	24	25	26	27	28
29	30	31				

MONTHLY GOALS

NEW GOALS TO FOCUS ON

WHAT WORKED LAST MONTH

WHAT COULD BE BETTER

Try to be a
RAINBOW
IN
someone's
CLOUD

AUGUST 2021

SUNDAY	MONDAY	TUESDAY	WEDNESDAY	THURSDAY	FRIDAY	SATURDAY
1	2 Summer Bank Holiday (SCT)	3	4	5	6	7
8	9	10	11	12	13	14
15	16	17	18	19	20	21
22	23	24	25	26	27	28
29	30 Summer Bank Holiday (UK except SCT)	31	1	2	3	4

CREATURE OF HABIT

Track new goals or habits and watch your progress every month!

HABIT	1	2	3	4	5	6	7	8	9	10	11	12	13	14	15	16	17	18	19	20	21	22	23	24	25	26	27	28	29	30	31

2021 AUGUST

MONDAY
2

Summer Bank Holiday (SCT)

TUESDAY
3

BE THE PERSON YOU DREAMED YOU WOULD BE, EVEN IF IT'S JUST TODAY.

WEDNESDAY
4

THURSDAY
5

START WHERE YOU ARE, NOT WHERE YOU THINK YOU SHOULD BE.

FRIDAY
6

WAVE YOUR SMILE AS YOUR OWN PERSONAL FLAG!

SATURDAY
7

SUNDAY
8

DON'T FORGET:

THIS WEEK'S
HAPPY MOMENT:

AUGUST 2021

S	M	T	W	T	F	S
1	2	3	4	5	6	7
8	9	10	11	12	13	14
15	16	17	18	19	20	21
22	23	24	25	26	27	28
29	30	31				

SEPTEMBER 2021

S	M	T	W	T	F	S
			1	2	3	4
5	6	7	8	9	10	11
12	13	14	15	16	17	18
19	20	21	22	23	24	25
26	27	28	29	30		

2021 **AUGUST**

MONDAY
9

TREAT YOURSELF WITH
THE LOVE YOU GIVE OTHERS.

TUESDAY
10

WEDNESDAY
11

CHANGE YOUR THINKING. CHANGE YOUR LIFE.

THURSDAY
12

IT'S A GOOD DAY TO HAVE A GOOD DAY!

FRIDAY 13

SATURDAY 14

YOU ARE MORE THAN GOOD ENOUGH.

SUNDAY 15

DON'T FORGET:

THIS WEEK'S HAPPY MOMENT:

AUGUST 2021

S	M	T	W	T	F	S
1	2	3	4	5	6	7
8	9	10	11	12	13	14
15	16	17	18	19	20	21
22	23	24	25	26	27	28
29	30	31				

SEPTEMBER 2021

S	M	T	W	T	F	S
			1	2	3	4
5	6	7	8	9	10	11
12	13	14	15	16	17	18
19	20	21	22	23	24	25
26	27	28	29	30		

2021 AUGUST

MONDAY
16

TUESDAY
17

KICK THAT FROWN OUT OF TOWN!

WEDNESDAY
18

THURSDAY
19

TOO MUCH OF A GOOD THING SOUNDS GREAT!

FRIDAY
20

LIFE DOESN'T
HAVE TO BE
PERFECT
TO BE
GLORIOUS.

SATURDAY
21

SUNDAY
22

DON'T FORGET:

THIS WEEK'S
HAPPY MOMENT:

AUGUST 2021

S	M	T	W	T	F	S
1	2	3	4	5	6	7
8	9	10	11	12	13	14
15	16	17	18	19	20	21
22	23	24	25	26	27	28
29	30	31				

SEPTEMBER 2021

S	M	T	W	T	F	S
			1	2	3	4
5	6	7	8	9	10	11
12	13	14	15	16	17	18
19	20	21	22	23	24	25
26	27	28	29	30		

MONDAY
23

TAKE ONE DAY AT A TIME.

TUESDAY
24

WEDNESDAY
25

YOU'RE BIGGER THAN YOUR TROUBLES.
THEY WON'T DEFEAT YOU.

THURSDAY
26

NO ONE IS TOO OLD FOR FAIRY TALES. IMMERSE YOURSELF IN A GOOD BOOK THIS WEEKEND.

FRIDAY 27

SATURDAY 28

SOMETIMES YOUR SMILE CAN BE THE SOURCE OF YOUR JOY.

SUNDAY 29

DON'T FORGET:

THIS WEEK'S HAPPY MOMENT:

AUGUST 2021

S	M	T	W	T	F	S
1	2	3	4	5	6	7
8	9	10	11	12	13	14
15	16	17	18	19	20	21
22	23	24	25	26	27	28
29	30	31				

SEPTEMBER 2021

S	M	T	W	T	F	S
			1	2	3	4
5	6	7	8	9	10	11
12	13	14	15	16	17	18
19	20	21	22	23	24	25
26	27	28	29	30		

MONTHLY GOALS

NEW GOALS TO FOCUS ON

WHAT WORKED LAST MONTH

WHAT COULD BE BETTER

WHEN LIFE
GETS BLURRY

ADJUST
YOUR FOCUS

SEPTEMBER 2021

SUNDAY	MONDAY	TUESDAY	WEDNESDAY	THURSDAY	FRIDAY	SATURDAY
29	30	31	1	2	3	4
5 Father's Day (AUS, NZ)	6 Labor Day (USA, CAN); Rosh Hashanah begins	7	8	9	10	11 Patriot Day
12	13	14	15 Yom Kippur begins	16	17	18
19	20 Sukkot begins	21	22 Autumn begins (Northern Hemisphere)	23	24	25
26	27	28	29	30	1	2

CREATURE OF HABIT

Track new goals or habits and watch your progress every month!

HABIT	1	2	3	4	5	6	7	8	9	10	11	12	13	14	15	16	17	18	19	20	21	22	23	24	25	26	27	28	29	30	31

2021 AUGUST/SEPTEMBER

MONDAY
30

Summer Bank Holiday (UK except SCT)

TUESDAY
31

WHO MATTERS MOST TO YOU? REMEMBER THAT YOU'RE IMPORTANT TO THEM TOO!

WEDNESDAY
1

THURSDAY
2

BIG THINGS OFTEN COME FROM SMALL BEGINNINGS.

FRIDAY
3

SATURDAY
4

FLEX YOUR CREATIVITY. YOUR BRAIN WILL THANK YOU!

SUNDAY
5

Father's Day (AUS, NZ)

DON'T FORGET:

THIS WEEK'S HAPPY MOMENT:

SEPTEMBER 2021

S	M	T	W	T	F	S
			1	2	3	4
5	6	7	8	9	10	11
12	13	14	15	16	17	18
19	20	21	22	23	24	25
26	27	28	29	30		

OCTOBER 2021

S	M	T	W	T	F	S
					1	2
3	4	5	6	7	8	9
10	11	12	13	14	15	16
17	18	19	20	21	22	23
24/31	25	26	27	28	29	30

2021 **SEPTEMBER**

MONDAY
6

LIFE. IS. GOOD.

Labor Day (USA, CAN); Rosh Hashanah begins

TUESDAY
7

WEDNESDAY
8

DON'T BE AFRAID TO BE GREAT.

THURSDAY
9

YOU ARE LIMITLESS.

FRIDAY
10

SATURDAY
11

Patriot Day

KNOW YOUR
WORTH!

SUNDAY
12

DON'T FORGET:

THIS WEEK'S
HAPPY MOMENT:

SEPTEMBER 2021

S	M	T	W	T	F	S
			1	2	3	4
5	6	7	8	9	10	11
12	13	14	15	16	17	18
19	20	21	22	23	24	25
26	27	28	29	30		

OCTOBER 2021

S	M	T	W	T	F	S
					1	2
3	4	5	6	7	8	9
10	11	12	13	14	15	16
17	18	19	20	21	22	23
24/31	25	26	27	28	29	30

MONDAY
13

TUESDAY
14

DWELL ON WHAT'S POSSIBLE.

WEDNESDAY
15

Yom Kippur begins

THURSDAY
16

GET OUT THERE AND
MAKE SOME MEMORIES!

FRIDAY
17

WHAT FANTASTIC THINGS ARE YOU GOING TO DO THIS WEEKEND?

SATURDAY
18

SUNDAY
19

DON'T FORGET:

THIS WEEK'S HAPPY MOMENT:

SEPTEMBER 2021

S	M	T	W	T	F	S
			1	2	3	4
5	6	7	8	9	10	11
12	13	14	15	16	17	18
19	20	21	22	23	24	25
26	27	28	29	30		

OCTOBER 2021

S	M	T	W	T	F	S
					1	2
3	4	5	6	7	8	9
10	11	12	13	14	15	16
17	18	19	20	21	22	23
24/31	25	26	27	28	29	30

MONDAY
20

A LITTLE KINDNESS CAN GO A LONG WAY.

Sukkot begins

TUESDAY
21

WEDNESDAY
22

SEEMS LIKE THE PERFECT DAY TO PLAY IN THE LEAVES!

Autumn begins (Northern Hemisphere)

THURSDAY
23

HAPPINESS IS NOT A STATE TO ARRIVE AT BUT A MANNER OF TRAVELING.

FRIDAY 24

SATURDAY 25

BE A GOOFBALL EVERY ONCE IN A WHILE.

SUNDAY 26

DON'T FORGET:

THIS WEEK'S HAPPY MOMENT:

SEPTEMBER 2021

S	M	T	W	T	F	S
			1	2	3	4
5	6	7	8	9	10	11
12	13	14	15	16	17	18
19	20	21	22	23	24	25
26	27	28	29	30		

OCTOBER 2021

S	M	T	W	T	F	S
					1	2
3	4	5	6	7	8	9
10	11	12	13	14	15	16
17	18	19	20	21	22	23
24/31	25	26	27	28	29	30

2021 SEPTEMBER/OCTOBER

MONDAY
27

TUESDAY
28

YOU'RE A MOVER AND A SHAKER!

WEDNESDAY
29

THURSDAY
30

KEEP LIVING YOUR BEST LIFE! YOU'VE GOT THIS.

FRIDAY
1

INDULGE IN A GUILTY PLEASURE TODAY, BUT DON'T FEEL GUILTY ABOUT IT!

SATURDAY
2

SUNDAY
3

DON'T FORGET:

THIS WEEK'S HAPPY MOMENT:

SEPTEMBER 2021

S	M	T	W	T	F	S
			1	2	3	4
5	6	7	8	9	10	11
12	13	14	15	16	17	18
19	20	21	22	23	24	25
26	27	28	29	30		

OCTOBER 2021

S	M	T	W	T	F	S
					1	2
3	4	5	6	7	8	9
10	11	12	13	14	15	16
17	18	19	20	21	22	23
24/31	25	26	27	28	29	30

MONTHLY GOALS

NEW GOALS TO FOCUS ON

WHAT WORKED LAST MONTH

WHAT COULD BE BETTER

EVERYTHING *Matters*
EVERYTHING *Counts*

OCTOBER 2021

SUNDAY	MONDAY	TUESDAY	WEDNESDAY	THURSDAY	FRIDAY	SATURDAY
26	27	28	29	30	1	2
3	4	5	6	7	8	9
10	11 Columbus Day (USA); Thanksgiving Day (CAN)	12	13	14	15	16
17	18	19	20	21	22	23
24/31 Halloween (31st)	25	26	27	28	29	30

CREATURE OF HABIT

Track new goals or habits and watch your progress every month!

HABIT	1	2	3	4	5	6	7	8	9	10	11	12	13	14	15	16	17	18	19	20	21	22	23	24	25	26	27	28	29	30	31

2021 OCTOBER

MONDAY
4

LIFE MOVES PRETTY FAST.
SLOW DOWN A MOMENT AND ENJOY IT!

TUESDAY
5

WEDNESDAY
6

FEELS LIKE AN AIR-GUITAR-SOLO KIND OF DAY!

THURSDAY
7

LITTLE THINGS CAN HAVE BIG IMPACTS.

FRIDAY 8

SATURDAY 9

ONLY GET DOWN ON THE DANCE FLOOR.

SUNDAY 10

DON'T FORGET:

OCTOBER 2021

S	M	T	W	T	F	S
					1	2
3	4	5	6	7	8	9
10	11	12	13	14	15	16
17	18	19	20	21	22	23
24/31	25	26	27	28	29	30

NOVEMBER 2021

S	M	T	W	T	F	S
	1	2	3	4	5	6
7	8	9	10	11	12	13
14	15	16	17	18	19	20
21	22	23	24	25	26	27
28	29	30				

THIS WEEK'S HAPPY MOMENT:

2021 OCTOBER

MONDAY
11

HELLO, MONDAY. LET'S MAKE IT HAPPEN!

Columbus Day (USA); Thanksgiving Day (CAN)

TUESDAY
12

WEDNESDAY
13

SPEED DOESN'T MATTER. FORWARD IS FORWARD.

THURSDAY
14

STRIVE TO BE PRESENT IN
EVERY ASPECT OF YOUR LIFE.

FRIDAY
15

SATURDAY
16

LOOK FOR THE GOOD IN
PEOPLE—AND YOURSELF.

SUNDAY
17

DON'T FORGET:

THIS WEEK'S
HAPPY MOMENT:

OCTOBER 2021

S	M	T	W	T	F	S
					1	2
3	4	5	6	7	8	9
10	11	12	13	14	15	16
17	18	19	20	21	22	23
24/31	25	26	27	28	29	30

NOVEMBER 2021

S	M	T	W	T	F	S
	1	2	3	4	5	6
7	8	9	10	11	12	13
14	15	16	17	18	19	20
21	22	23	24	25	26	27
28	29	30				

2021 **OCTOBER**

MONDAY
18

TUESDAY
19

BE BOLD. BE HONEST. BE BRAVE.

WEDNESDAY
20

THURSDAY
21

MAKE SILLY FACES. THEY WON'T
STAY LIKE THAT FOREVER!

FRIDAY
22

YOU ARE
LOVED.

SATURDAY
23

SUNDAY
24

DON'T FORGET:

THIS WEEK'S
HAPPY MOMENT:

OCTOBER 2021

S	M	T	W	T	F	S
					1	2
3	4	5	6	7	8	9
10	11	12	13	14	15	16
17	18	19	20	21	22	23
24/31	25	26	27	28	29	30

NOVEMBER 2021

S	M	T	W	T	F	S
	1	2	3	4	5	6
7	8	9	10	11	12	13
14	15	16	17	18	19	20
21	22	23	24	25	26	27
28	29	30				

2021 OCTOBER

MONDAY
25

YOU CAN MAKE TODAY AMAZING
IF YOU WANT TO!

TUESDAY
26

WEDNESDAY
27

DECISIONS DETERMINE DESTINY.

THURSDAY
28

GIVE A STRANGER A COMPLIMENT. YOU'LL BOTH FEEL GREAT!

FRIDAY 29

SATURDAY 30

WE ALL HAVE A LITTLE BIT OF MAGIC INSIDE US.

SUNDAY 31

Halloween

DON'T FORGET:

THIS WEEK'S HAPPY MOMENT:

OCTOBER 2021

S	M	T	W	T	F	S
					1	2
3	4	5	6	7	8	9
10	11	12	13	14	15	16
17	18	19	20	21	22	23
24/31	25	26	27	28	29	30

NOVEMBER 2021

S	M	T	W	T	F	S
	1	2	3	4	5	6
7	8	9	10	11	12	13
14	15	16	17	18	19	20
21	22	23	24	25	26	27
28	29	30				

MONTHLY GOALS

NEW GOALS TO FOCUS ON

WHAT WORKED LAST MONTH

WHAT COULD BE BETTER

yes
you
can

NOVEMBER 2021

SUNDAY	MONDAY	TUESDAY	WEDNESDAY	THURSDAY	FRIDAY	SATURDAY
31	1	2 Election Day	3	4 Diwali begins	5	6
7 Daylight Saving Time ends (USA, CAN)	8	9	10	11 Veterans Day (USA); Remembrance Day (CAN, UK)	12	13
14	15	16	17	18	19	20
21	22	23	24	25 Thanksgiving Day	26	27
28 Hanukkah begins	29	30 St. Andrew's Day (SCT)	1	2	3	4

CREATURE OF HABIT

Track new goals or habits and watch your progress every month!

HABIT	1	2	3	4	5	6	7	8	9	10	11	12	13	14	15	16	17	18	19	20	21	22	23	24	25	26	27	28	29	30	31

2021 **NOVEMBER**

MONDAY
1

TUESDAY
2

HAPPINESS IS A HABIT.

Election Day

WEDNESDAY
3

THURSDAY
4

TREAT YOURSELF TO THAT
FANCY COFFEE. YOU DESERVE IT!

Diwali begins

FRIDAY
5

SATURDAY
6

IT'S NOT
WHAT
YOU LOOK
AT THAT
MATTERS.
IT'S WHAT
YOU SEE.

SUNDAY
7

Daylight Saving Time ends (USA, CAN)

DON'T FORGET:

THIS WEEK'S
HAPPY MOMENT:

NOVEMBER 2021

S	M	T	W	T	F	S
	1	2	3	4	5	6
7	8	9	10	11	12	13
14	15	16	17	18	19	20
21	22	23	24	25	26	27
28	29	30				

DECEMBER 2021

S	M	T	W	T	F	S
			1	2	3	4
5	6	7	8	9	10	11
12	13	14	15	16	17	18
19	20	21	22	23	24	25
26	27	28	29	30	31	

2021 **NOVEMBER**

MONDAY
8

BEING HAPPY NEVER GOES OUT OF STYLE. FLAUNT IT!

TUESDAY
9

WEDNESDAY
10

BE A VOICE, NOT AN ECHO.

THURSDAY
11

Veterans Day (USA); Remembrance Day (CAN, UK)

MAKE SOMEONE LAUGH OUT LOUD, AND LAUGH WITH THEM!

FRIDAY 12

SATURDAY 13

KEEP HANGING IN THERE!

SUNDAY 14

DON'T FORGET:

THIS WEEK'S HAPPY MOMENT:

NOVEMBER 2021

S	M	T	W	T	F	S
	1	2	3	4	5	6
7	8	9	10	11	12	13
14	15	16	17	18	19	20
21	22	23	24	25	26	27
28	29	30				

DECEMBER 2021

S	M	T	W	T	F	S
			1	2	3	4
5	6	7	8	9	10	11
12	13	14	15	16	17	18
19	20	21	22	23	24	25
26	27	28	29	30	31	

2021 NOVEMBER

MONDAY
15

TUESDAY
16

JUST BEGIN.

WEDNESDAY
17

THURSDAY
18

NOTHING TURNS A BAD MOOD INTO A GOOD ONE LIKE CHOCOLATE.

FRIDAY
19

LOVE IS ALL
YOU NEED.

SATURDAY
20

SUNDAY
21

DON'T FORGET:

THIS WEEK'S
HAPPY MOMENT:

NOVEMBER 2021

S	M	T	W	T	F	S
	1	2	3	4	5	6
7	8	9	10	11	12	13
14	15	16	17	18	19	20
21	22	23	24	25	26	27
28	29	30				

DECEMBER 2021

S	M	T	W	T	F	S
			1	2	3	4
5	6	7	8	9	10	11
12	13	14	15	16	17	18
19	20	21	22	23	24	25
26	27	28	29	30	31	

MONDAY
22

CONGRATULATIONS! YOU'RE WINNING AT LIFE!

TUESDAY
23

WEDNESDAY
24

WHAT ARE YOU GRATEFUL FOR? DON'T FORGET TO INCLUDE YOURSELF!

THURSDAY
25

Thanksgiving Day

EAT, DRINK, AND BE THANKFUL!

FRIDAY
26

SATURDAY
27

JUST ENJOY
WHERE YOU
ARE NOW.

SUNDAY
28

Hanukkah begins

DON'T FORGET:

THIS WEEK'S
HAPPY MOMENT:

NOVEMBER 2021

S	M	T	W	T	F	S
	1	2	3	4	5	6
7	8	9	10	11	12	13
14	15	16	17	18	19	20
21	22	23	24	25	26	27
28	29	30				

DECEMBER 2021

S	M	T	W	T	F	S
			1	2	3	4
5	6	7	8	9	10	11
12	13	14	15	16	17	18
19	20	21	22	23	24	25
26	27	28	29	30	31	

MONTHLY GOALS

NEW GOALS TO FOCUS ON

WHAT WORKED LAST MONTH

WHAT COULD BE BETTER

Do small Things with great Love

DECEMBER 2021

SUNDAY	MONDAY	TUESDAY	WEDNESDAY	THURSDAY	FRIDAY	SATURDAY
28	29	30	1	2	3	4
5	6	7 Pearl Harbor Day	8	9	10	11
12	13	14	15	16	17	18
19	20	21 Winter begins (Northern Hemisphere)	22	23	24 Christmas Eve	25 Christmas Day
26 Kwanzaa begins; Boxing Day (AUS, CAN, NZ, UK)	27	28	29	30	31 New Year's Eve	1

CREATURE OF HABIT

Track new goals or habits and watch your progress every month!

HABIT	1	2	3	4	5	6	7	8	9	10	11	12	13	14	15	16	17	18	19	20	21	22	23	24	25	26	27	28	29	30	31

2021 NOVEMBER/DECEMBER

MONDAY
29

TUESDAY
30

COLLECT EXPERIENCES, NOT THINGS.

St. Andrew's Day (SCT)

WEDNESDAY
1

THURSDAY
2

GO AT YOUR OWN PACE.

FRIDAY
3

NOTHING MAKES
A GREAT NIGHT
LIKE TAKEOUT
AND YOUR
FAVORITE MOVIE.
ENJOY IT!

SATURDAY
4

SUNDAY
5

DON'T FORGET:

THIS WEEK'S
HAPPY MOMENT:

DECEMBER 2021

S	M	T	W	T	F	S
			1	2	3	4
5	6	7	8	9	10	11
12	13	14	15	16	17	18
19	20	21	22	23	24	25
26	27	28	29	30	31	

JANUARY 2022

S	M	T	W	T	F	S
						1
2	3	4	5	6	7	8
9	10	11	12	13	14	15
16	17	18	19	20	21	22
23/30	24/31	25	26	27	28	29

2021 DECEMBER

MONDAY
6

DO YOU KNOW YOU DON'T HAVE TO MEET EVERYONE'S EXPECTATIONS?

TUESDAY
7

Pearl Harbor Day

WEDNESDAY
8

ALL ABOARD THE POSITIVITY TRAIN!

THURSDAY
9

IT DOESN'T MAKE YOU WEAK TO NEED A LITTLE ENCOURAGEMENT.

FRIDAY 10

SATURDAY 11

HAVE SOME FUN TODAY. THAT'S AN ORDER!

SUNDAY 12

DON'T FORGET:

THIS WEEK'S HAPPY MOMENT:

DECEMBER 2021

S	M	T	W	T	F	S
			1	2	3	4
5	6	7	8	9	10	11
12	13	14	15	16	17	18
19	20	21	22	23	24	25
26	27	28	29	30	31	

JANUARY 2022

S	M	T	W	T	F	S
						1
2	3	4	5	6	7	8
9	10	11	12	13	14	15
16	17	18	19	20	21	22
23/30	24/31	25	26	27	28	29

2021 DECEMBER

MONDAY
13

TUESDAY
14

EVERY DAY IS AN OPPORTUNITY
TO LEARN SOMETHING NEW.

WEDNESDAY
15

THURSDAY
16

SMILES ARE ALWAYS TRENDING!

FRIDAY
17

IN A WORLD
WHERE YOU
CAN BE
ANYTHING,
BE KIND.

SATURDAY
18

SUNDAY
19

DON'T FORGET:

THIS WEEK'S
HAPPY MOMENT:

DECEMBER 2021

S	M	T	W	T	F	S
			1	2	3	4
5	6	7	8	9	10	11
12	13	14	15	16	17	18
19	20	21	22	23	24	25
26	27	28	29	30	31	

JANUARY 2022

S	M	T	W	T	F	S
						1
2	3	4	5	6	7	8
9	10	11	12	13	14	15
16	17	18	19	20	21	22
23/30	24/31	25	26	27	28	29

2021 DECEMBER

MONDAY
20

'TIS THE SEASON TO BE JOYFUL!

TUESDAY
21

Winter begins (Northern Hemisphere)

WEDNESDAY
22

EVEN ON THE DARKEST DAY,
REMEMBER YOU CAN SHINE!

THURSDAY
23

YOU'RE THE BEST PRESENT
UNDER THAT TREE!

FRIDAY
24

Christmas Eve

SATURDAY
25

Christmas Day

FIND YOUR ZEN.

SUNDAY
26

Kwanzaa begins; Boxing Day (AUS, CAN, NZ, UK)

DON'T FORGET:

THIS WEEK'S
HAPPY MOMENT:

DECEMBER 2021

S	M	T	W	T	F	S
			1	2	3	4
5	6	7	8	9	10	11
12	13	14	15	16	17	18
19	20	21	22	23	24	25
26	27	28	29	30	31	

JANUARY 2022

S	M	T	W	T	F	S
						1
2	3	4	5	6	7	8
9	10	11	12	13	14	15
16	17	18	19	20	21	22
23/30	24/31	25	26	27	28	29

MONDAY
27

TUESDAY
28

NEVER FORGET ALL IT TOOK FOR YOU TO BE HERE. CELEBRATE!

WEDNESDAY
29

THURSDAY
30

WHAT ARE YOU MOST LOOKING FORWARD TO IN 2022? GET EXCITED!

FRIDAY
31

New Year's Eve

YOUR GRADE IN AWESOMENESS THIS YEAR: A+

SATURDAY
1

New Year's Day

SUNDAY
2

Day after New Year's Day (NZ, SCT)

DON'T FORGET:

THIS WEEK'S HAPPY MOMENT:

DECEMBER 2021

S	M	T	W	T	F	S
			1	2	3	4
5	6	7	8	9	10	11
12	13	14	15	16	17	18
19	20	21	22	23	24	25
26	27	28	29	30	31	

JANUARY 2022

S	M	T	W	T	F	S
						1
2	3	4	5	6	7	8
9	10	11	12	13	14	15
16	17	18	19	20	21	22
23/30	24/31	25	26	27	28	29

NOTES AND INSPIRATION

Cover and internal design by Brittany Vibbert/Sourcebooks
Cover and internal images © Talirina/Shutterstock, BlueLela/iStockphoto, pa3x/Shutterstock, Weape Studio/Shutterstock, Elen Koss/Shutterstock, freepik.com, Utro_na_more/iStockphoto, InnaPoka/iStockphoto, Olga Zakharova/iStockphoto, pikisuperstar, tasza_natasha/iStockphoto, Yulia337/iStockphoto,

Jewish and Muslim holidays begin at sundown.

Published by Sourcebooks.
P.O. Box 4410, Naperville, Illinois 60567-4410
(630) 961-3900
sourcebooks.com

Printed and bound in Singapore.
OGP 10 9 8 7 6 5 4 3 2 1

APPOINTMENT

APPOINTMENT

APPOINTMENT

APPOINTMENT

APPOINTMENT

APPOINTMENT

APPOINTMENT

APPOINTMENT

APPOINTMENT

APPOINTMENT

APPOINTMENT

APPOINTMENT

MEETING

MEETING

MEETING

MEETING

MEETING

MEETING

MEETING

MEETING

MEETING

MEETING

MEETING

BIRTHDAY!

BIRTHDAY!

BIRTHDAY!

BIRTHDAY!

BIRTHDAY!

Stay Strong BE Positive

Explore MORE

YOU ARE ENOUGH

NOTE TO SELF

NOTE TO SELF

NOTE TO SELF

NOTE TO SELF

NOTE TO SELF

NOTE TO SELF

NOTE TO SELF

NOTE TO SELF

NOTE TO SELF

NOTE TO SELF

NOTE TO SELF

NOTE TO SELF

APPOINTMENT

APPOINTMENT

APPOINTMENT

APPOINTMENT

APPOINTMENT

APPOINTMENT

APPOINTMENT

APPOINTMENT

APPOINTMENT

APPOINTMENT

APPOINTMENT

PLANS

PLANS

PLANS

PLANS

PLANS

PLANS

PLANS

PLANS

PLANS

PLANS

PLANS

BIRTHDAY!

BIRTHDAY!

BIRTHDAY!

BIRTHDAY!

BIRTHDAY!

WORK HARD STAY STRONG

everything WILL BE okay

BE HAPPY

DUE DATE!

DUE DATE!

DUE DATE!

DUE DATE!

DUE DATE!

DUE DATE!

DUE DATE!

DUE DATE!

DUE DATE!

DUE DATE!

DUE DATE!

DUE DATE!

CELEBRATE!

PLANS

BIRTHDAY!

GOOD VIBES

CELEBRATE!

PLANS

CELEBRATE!

PLANS

BIRTHDAY!

DAY OFF

DAY OFF

CELEBRATE!

PLANS

CELEBRATE!

PLANS

DAY OFF

DAY OFF

CELEBRATE!

PLANS

BIRTHDAY!

CELEBRATE!

PLANS

DAY OFF

DAY OFF

CELEBRATE!

PLANS

BIRTHDAY!

CELEBRATE!

PLANS

DAY OFF

DAY OFF

CELEBRATE!

PLANS

CELEBRATE!

PLANS

BIRTHDAY!

DAY OFF

DAY OFF

CELEBRATE!

PLANS

BIRTHDAY!

DUE DATE!

DUE DATE!

DUE DATE!

DUE DATE!

DUE DATE!

DUE DATE!

DUE DATE!

DUE DATE!

DUE DATE!

DUE DATE!

DUE DATE!

DUE DATE!

HOORAY!
HOORAY!
HOORAY!
HOORAY!
HOORAY!
HOORAY!
SELF CARE
SELF CARE
SELF CARE
SELF CARE
SELF CARE
SELF CARE
SELF CARE
SELF CARE
SELF CARE
SELF CARE
SELF CARE
SELF CARE
PACK your THINGS
get LOST
TRAVEL
PACK your THINGS
DREAM IT. PLAN IT. DO IT.
TRAVEL
PACK your THINGS
get LOST
TRAVEL
REFRESH
REFRESH
REFRESH
Make TODAY GREAT
TREAT YO' SELF!
TREAT YO' SELF!